Worked Stiff
Poetry and Prose For the Common

Written By
Marc D. Crepeaux

Art By
Mads Bender

-Disclaimer-

The information in this book is meant to supplement, not replace, actual Work. Like any sport involving speed, equipment, balance and environmental factors, Work poses some inherent risk. The author, illustrator and publisher advise readers to take full responsibility for their safety and know their limits. Before practicing the skills described in this book, be sure that your equipment is well maintained, and do not take risks beyond your level of experience, aptitude, training, and comfort level.

This book is a work of fiction. Names, characters, places, and incidents either are products of the author's imagination or are used fictitiously. Any resemblance to actual persons, living or dead, events, or locales is entirely coincidental.

For Kimberly, a woman who holds in her hand a slice of the true American Dream.
Despite all odds, she worked with supreme diligence, raised two boys and supported
their many professions. Above all, thank you for shaping my life Mom.
-Marc

I owe my vision to Jessica who helps me see all things and keeps the light on the path
so we can always see where we are going.
-Mads

Contents

WELCO
HOM

Forward

This collection is a salute and celebration of the modern American worker. Generations of unrecognized heroes who wash our cars, mow our lawns, bake our bread, douse our fires, take out our garbage, teach our kids, grow our food, build our houses, mend our roads, and defend our freedom. Some who dare to read this collection may end up, heaven forbid, pondering a little about the world and other people around them. If that does occur, you may think or even say aloud to somebody who pretends to care for the moment: "Hey, this here is all just a big whine- a real bleeding heart liberal squawking, I must stop reading at once! Can you believe this guy?" Some may even believe the opposite to be true, that surely the writer involving himself in these works is a big-government hating, non-taxpaying conservative thug, or even a libertarian, of all things, who wants nothing more than to take away all taxes and programs that would assist the working class in any way whatsoever. "This guy, this Frenchie, is a wanna –be Neo-Con with the preemptive strike of a free-market loving lunatic! Where did he come from?" I ask you to leave these notions of judgement at the door please. Take them off like clothes, you'll feel better, trust me.

Just hold tight there-Rooster, I'm an American, true blue. You won't be able to pin me down. Besides, we wouldn't want to jump to any conclusions and start the pecking right off anyway. After all, that's what they want.

Now, I know that it is very easy to say the word they to your friends as it pretty much defines whoever is against you at the time of retched thought or hopeless debate. For some, they is meant to describe the overpowering menace of G-Men and their alien lizard warlords who run the show. For others, it's Oprah Winfrey, philanthropy in general, the contradictory hordes that pretend to care for others, people who drive a Prius, or those who have a vegetable garden that they like to meddle in, later listening to NPR and drinking chamomile. That's who they must surely be.

For me and my purposes, they are who is in power in today's American economic and political machine. As a surprise for many, the powerful and elite have their little diablo hooves on both sides of the political spectrum. Really??? Yes, all can be found wearing the cloaks of Republicans, Democrats and everything in between and on either side of the extreme.

"They're all crooks-downright, no-good liars," my father once said of politicians, and I believed him. I believed him because at one point in their careers, the politicians who now run the show surely must have compromised their integrity at one point or another. The first transgression could have even been early on, in order to win that mayoral race way back when. It could be that it happened only recently. Your guy or gal stuck to their guns for the majority of their political career, not to be bought by anyone, yet when it came to the big race, they had to bow to the real powers that be: The teams they were playing for and the money behind them. These teams can be tricky too, even choose with coin amongst them, who is best suited to win against the opposition and all that. After they are all good and compromised with regards to integrity, what many of them do is take one issue, maybe two, often social, because social issues get the most fire from the bellies of the people. They go ahead and nicely define the sides of the political debate for you.

If one team's mascot says oh they just love the color purple, they will do absolutely anything in their power to defend the right to purple. The other side's mascot says that purple is what is wrong with America, but BOTH sides take on floods of money illegally and legally from anybody who will doll it out, regardless of their stance on purple. These politicians do this for future favors, in the form of policy decisions, which also don't have anything to do with purple or the safety thereof. To top it off, neither side wants to do anything about purple during their term because it may rock the boat and they are counting on votes and money from both pro-purple and anti-purple sides that stray away from their main flagpole for their own petty reasons altogether. Like they don't appreciate her hair, or he doesn't stand presidential or something like that. So the issue of purple becomes a non-issue in the campaign and in the time of rule, yet, everybody gets so crazy over the color anyway, drawing lines in the sand when it doesn't actually matter. That's all a big distraction. What matters is money, food on the table. People vote for or against purple despite the fact that everyone involved is ignoring the plight of the modern middle-class and the American worker.

People throw their votes away on one or a few stand-alone issues while they are being robbed blind. This game we are playing is rigged. The American Dream is, well, different. I think it's a tad cliché to say that The American Dream is dead, besides, I don't believe it. The dream is still there, hidden in plain sight, riddled with confusion and abandonment. This game we are playing is chaotic, and the league we are playing in, the system, well, it's broken. Think I am wrong? Just search-however you want-old-school in the library or new-wave on the interwebs for the difference in salary of the middle-class from 1950-NOW. How about the difference in salary of the top 1%? Have you or someone you know been in need of a job lately? Talking about the wage gap has become a political issue, when it just shouldn't be, what we are talking about is facts. Think statistics lie? Sure they do, but I can tell you that counting does not lie.

Yes, ever since my high chair days, counting has been solid evidence of either having or not having something. I can tell you that for most people in America, they are on the unfortunate side of not-having when it comes to jobs, a solid, steady wage, and a future that looks bright for their children. Those early days of counting macaroni didn't even fathom negative counting, otherwise known as debt. Debt has been around as long as there has been a form of currency, but not in my country. Mortgage? Student loans? Credit Cards? These evils, only generations ago, didn't even exist in America, yet they are used oh so cleverly to fill in the gap of what workers should be actually earning compared to what they have been left with.

Does that mean that a rich man who climbed his way to the top is undeserving? No, actually, I don't believe that at all. Well, what about some tight wad whose family struck oil and he inherited the world on a silver platter? Good for him, I say, hope he was raised well and he knows what to do with all that cheddar. You see, I don't have envy. I do want to be wealthy too, though. Who wouldn't at least want the opportunity for advancement? Advancement may not just mean money either, for some it can mean education, opportunity to travel, home ownership, or simply freedom of time.

Who I absolutely hate is the winner of the climbing contest that cuts the rope behind him so that nobody else has the chance to match or beat his record, and he has no fear of going back down the rope again. I loathe the man who makes it past the gate of wealth and opportunity, only to barricade the castle walls with guards, archers, a drawbridge, moat and sharks with lasers to protect his position. I hate the politician who got elected with his own money and that of a few friends, only to enact policy solely to protect both growing piles. Will they starve all of a sudden if they think about the future of America over their own bottom line? No, certainly not. Plenty of wealthy men and women throughout history have provided the opportunity for advancement to other human beings without being worse for the wear. Notice I said, opportunity for advancement and not handout? Unfortunately, some amongst us on both sides of the aisle refuse to recognize the difference.

I quoted my father earlier, and I'll do it again, because everyone should listen to their parents on occasion: "You have to keep an open mind, son." This is pretty easy to say, and actually, pretty easy to do.

So read on and enjoy with an open mind the celebration, story, and circumstance of the modern American worker and all the small yet wonderful moments that make up our lives. And please remember that your hands are only as clean as the towel you dry them on.

– Marc

Must Be Trash

I was born and grew into a world with two moms and two dads. I have a big family and they don't necessarily all talk to each other. They all love me though, I must be trash.

We lived for a spell in two trailers, paid in cash. First a single wide and then upgraded to a double on the same piece of land, renting out the smaller. Then, my parents broke through the lower-middle class ceiling and we bought a house, a real house. We must have been trash.

I learned how to work early from my fathers, I always had a job. I felt great pride while holding my working papers for the first time outside the county courthouse at the age of fourteen. I also had a library card, I was official. I must have been trash.

I watched as my two fathers and one mother lost their jobs, a result of globalization, the undercutting of American know-how and the overwhelming concern for the industrial bottom line. This scarred me for life and has since fueled my vision to make a living that does not rely on one company with forty years of my undying devotion. I must be trash.

I left that crumbling town for the pursuit of something bigger and altogether unachievable. This has never stopped me from trying though, and I will always be dreaming of something better for me and my children. I must be trash.

I signed up with Uncle Sam and he treated me like a doll. This level of suffering taught me to recognize what I have and forget about what I don't. This is called prioritization. Time spent in this fashion has given me a clear understanding of what I should and should not hold dear. I believe that all young men and women should suffer in order to overcome pettiness in their lives early and to maintain an understanding of happiness as it comes to them. I must be trash.

I bought a ragged house in an unconventional way and spent five months making it into a home with blood, worry and sweat. I learned a lot about the world, myself, and home ownership during that time. I consulted my two fathers daily, I must have been trash.

I built a business from nothing, failed, and did it again. I am a proud owner of a meager operation which employs a handful of men and women in a low-brow industry. They can look at themselves through a steamy mirror in the morning and know that dinner is going to happen that night. I must be trash.

I am a shaper, a creative leader yet a manager grounded in logic. I am also smart enough to recognize that empire is the true American Dream, I must be trash.

I find working for someone else to be overall less enjoyable that making it on your own. The concept of someone giving you a job is ridiculous. This is America, land of the entrepreneurs, men and women with vision. I must be trash.

I recognize a bad situation when I see one. There is no silver bullet in this economy and I remain uncertain of what I want to be when I grow up. That I feel is ok, I must be trash.

I like to get dirty, fix my own car when I can and feel real soil between my hands when I plant a crop. Everybody should chop wood on occasion. I want my children to feel the same level of accomplishment, I must be trash.

I have an appreciation for the country, the fresh air straight from a thick forest hitting my overburdened lungs and a frog pond to test your luck and do some fishing in. I must be trash.

I prefer real food, from real people, or greens that I can grow myself. I have my own suspicions regarding modern medicine, it killed my grandmother. I must be trash.

I maintain a loose moral code which remains situational. I will not judge and there is not a whole lot anybody can say that would surprise or outright offend me. I am unassuming, I must be trash.

I can eat with chopsticks, speak another language, and I continue the pursuit of academic achievement regardless of the cost. Knowledge is power and education should be free. This is all fake, printed money anyway, I must be trash.

I like to tell a tall-tale, embellish on the facts to meet your needs yet I have an undeniable hunger for the truth. This is one of many dualities of all men. We haven't got a lot of time left in this world so we might as well make our interactions entertaining. I must be trash.

I want to live simply and produce more than I consume. I am always thinking about how to better myself and the world around me. I do have my demons though; they plague all of us, the darkness hidden within. I also recognize the importance of technology in this era of humanity. I can envision a live and let live world with cut-down bureaucracy, access to knowledge in every home, and an appreciation for nature without destroying her on a daily basis. This, I feel, is a solid dream. I must be trash.

The Dreaded Interview

I see that you are wearing new shoes.
Did you buy them just for this interview?
Did you think you were going to get a job here?
Well then, you may have come to the right place.
Sit down, sit down.

Where is your paperwork?
Ah, here it is, here it is. I have it after all.
Seems to be a little missing.
Seems to be a little empty.
Have you conquered any challenges lately? No?

You don't have to fidget while sitting there.
That chair will hold you just fine.
Would you like something to chew on?
I am going to smoke, do you mind if I smoke?
Would you like a smoke? Not yet, ok.

How long have you been standing outside?
How long did it take you to get here?

Are you looking for a job?

What job do you feel you are best qualified for?

Oh yes, the only job we have available.

There is no real job here.

Only a mundane task in a sense.

Can you hold my sweater?

Good, glad you could do that at least.

Says here you have worked in dungeons before.

We have a dungeon here too.

Look around, you are so lucky.

There were thousands of applicants.

We picked yours at random.

Can we count on you?

Don't worry about a thing on your first day.

When can you start? Tomorrow?

You'll start tomorrow.

But I don't know what you'll be doing exactly.

Do you? Well...do you?

That is why you are here!

You must help us figure out what we are hiring for.

The dust in here eats at everyone who works here.

The halls echo too, you must watch out for that.
When can you start? Tomorrow?

We have spent a long time,
Looking for a proper candidate.
How long? Days.
But we haven't hired in quite a number of years.
What is the job exactly? We don't know yet.

I am glad you drank your water so quickly.
I am glad you came at the correct time.
I am glad you wore those nice new shoes.
You are hired but the halls still echo, remember that.
Our time here is complete.

Bankruptcy

More often than not, it happens with your own rupture.

Your spending begins to bust at the seams, one small catastrophe after another.

You know you won't be able to live so fancy.

You wonder, will anyone bring notification?

Will they come to your company?

Will they take your car right from the employee lot and tell your supervisor?

Nights become sleepless, knuckles cracked.

All you can do is admit your guilt in the situation.

You have lived your life to the fullest, and until now, without penalty.

It is time to pay for your sins and make a declaration.

In seven years, you will be fine. In seven years, you will be a completely new person.

No one will ever know.

Tax

"Capitalism failed! Capitalism failed!" The growing hoards cry.
"See? We knew all along, those greedy money-makers always got the best!"
"One hundred years! One hundred years since the gap has been this great!"
"The government should do something!" Men and Women stamp and stomp.
But they are fighting for the wrong cause, they are barking up the wrong tree.
"The government should do something! The government should do something!"

I turn my head only for a moment, and then continue to work.
I work for a negative number. My number is negative.
This was not the owner's intention.
My boss on the floor of the factory didn't want this for me, for us.
But I think I know why, I think I know where:

Sales Tax
Withholding Tax
Corporation Tax
Property Tax
School Tax
Estate transfer Tax
Metropolitan Commuter Tax
Estimated Tax
Fiduciary Tax
Gains Tax
Hazardous Waste Tax
Highway Use Tax
Fuel Use Tax
Alcoholic Beverages Tax
Cigarette and Tobacco Tax
Miscellaneous Tax
Motor Fuel Tax
Non-Specific Tax
Pari-Mutuel Tax
Public Safety Communications Tax
Real Estate Transfer Tax

Mortgage Recording Tax
Stock Transfer Tax
Waste Tire Management Tax
Payroll Tax
Luxury Tax
City Tax
Federal Tax
Death Tax

Some of these can be escaped, some cannot.
Some I can choose, but most aren't meant to be chosen.
Some I pay direct, some come out in a trickle.
Same as a frog being boiled from lukewarm in a pot.
Some are for the common good, others hide behind that heroic shield.

There is one that leaves me feeling most helpless and alone:

Income Tax

This tax is a hedged bet on my capabilities.
This is a tax on my success.
This tax is calculated carefully by my sweat and tears.
This tax doesn't care how hard or how long the fight took.
This tax is based on my own creative output.
This tax is based on hours of my life.
This tax is imbalanced so that success means failure.
This tax has been paid in pain and sorrow.
This tax has been handed over by empty moments, brainless frustration.
The more this tax bleeds away, the less chance for reciprocation.

What's Next? Campaign Tax? Rocket Ship Tax? Stealth Tax? Or, perhaps we could have a new Peanut Tax? A Protest Tax? Weeds In My Yard Tax? Tree Tax? Fancy Tax? Drab Tax? Fashion Tax? Sex Tax? Pregnant Tax? Blind Tax? Thinking Tax? Complaint Tax? Pain Tax? Reflective Tax?

I never quite seem to get what I have earned.
I never seem to make enough.
I never seem to make too little.

I am unsure of the purpose.
I am unsure of the proceeds.
I never asked for a handout.

I have worried.
I have waited.
I have thought.

I want it all back.

Bureaucracy

You devilish figure in multiple stale disguises.
You wait on us with glossy name tags,
over bitten fingernails and stacks of paper.
You breed lazy drones that hide behind rules.

You are a machine that works, yes.
Yet, your function requires far too many components,
clicking, clacking, pretending to be modular.
The left hand never utters a decision to the right.

Go to this one, to here, no. Go to that, yes, they can help you.
Apparently, our job is to bridge the gap,
step into another long line with the best of intentions.
Politely smile because we secretly enjoy playing your game.

You attempt to crush our spirit, wanting to, without ever being sure why.
Are we supposed to give up now? Are we supposed to go away?
Drivel and melancholy, you hate your life too, we see common ground.
How does anybody get anything done around here?

Even if we can solve your organized puzzle,
Even if we can fill out your forms, check all the boxes,
you are not fit for victory, nobody makes it this far.
We enjoy the challenge, the execution of request.

Being legitimate becomes unnecessary.
Perhaps working yourself out of a job is the whole point.
Manager to read to us slowly out of a book of restrictions.
Read to us in their soft robotic voice the salty justifications for 'no.'

Then, we can depart to our comfortable homes,
figure our way around your existence.
It will be great, have faith. You won't even have to work.

Out There, Workin'

The early beating drums,
rounded dirt in the webs and cracks of
yesterday's fingers and callused hands.
The foreman called 'em off the line.
Yeah, we were out there, workin'.

Later, a sounding crash,
only a hiccup in the drone,
stopped only a few,
those chip counters in the office, maybe.
But we were out there anyway, workin'.

A news flash appeared,
"planes run into by buildings," or something like that.
Places where decisions were made that
affected us all, none of us understood.
We were out there, workin'.

Eddy teared up a little
after looking over his shoulder,
but I swear he didn't stop swinging that hammer.
When the call was made to drop those monoliths,
we were out there, workin'.

When the big G decided to bail out
every banker in a three-piece,
and leave us holdin' the bill
to pass on to our kids, a lasting legacy of the faded,
we were out there, workin'.

When the snow caps started to melt,
or didn't.
When the funny-made crops of one company's vision
of the future caused cancer,
or didn't.
When some protectionists decided NOT to have
America lead industry away from fossil fuels,
we were out there, workin'.

When votes became a form of currency,
and only a few had enough tokens.
When those who could afford to play,
began to define policy for everybody,
we were out there, workin'

Somebody got a wild hair, sought to make a killing,
and sort of declared war, as it were, not sure what they call it now,
but our sons and daughters headed out.
Some paid the ultimate price, some still do in their beds.
They left and a many of their friends didn't come back,
while we were out there, workin'.

It started with our fathers,
they closed down this plant, moved that.
We prayed in the shuffle,
while our spending tried to stay the same,
our income lessened.

When they close 'em all down for good,
and we die holdin' on to turmoil and a stiff IOU,
our ghosts will be out there, workin'.

On Immigration

GO ahead, let them right on in! Find them, save them if the need be!
"Give us your tired, your poor..." as Emma etched on the Colossus' tablet.
Bring them to the fold-legit like, even make it easier-processed and ready for exploitation.
Just like the Irish coming off the boats with a belly full of famine.
Handed a musket and a pretty navy uniform with a valuable promise-a golden parchment.
Their families would be fine-just fine while they were gone-their children's children would prosper.
All they had to do was defend their new nation's fertile lands from those other mics in the South.

No need to dwell in the past though, for genius occurs both there and in the future.
No need to treat the newfound hopesters nice either.
Exploit their dreams and give them a real solid promise for their next generation.
Hand those wanderers a blank check that's never been signed.
Huge too, like the soon to be destructors that win the lotto, indoctrinate to the fullest.
After all, that promise is backed by a bloated bank account- and only the biggest will do.

No one can handle the wholesome, solid dream of a better life without a spoonful of suffering.
Who on this rock would give away such freedom and prosperity without cost?
No one would appreciate such a kind, selfless act.
The expectant must earn even mild success by swallowing the big slippery pill that is America.
For years this medicine has gone down millions of hatches and produced miraculous results.
America is the ugly truth-the mirrored reflection of the world.

Humankind looks at the confused, mongrel offspring and wants in-
Test the experiment again and again.
America -the petri dish-the only decent place for the hopeless and disenchanted.
Sufferers of the world must be allowed to unite in one low point and dig in.
Players need to come from behind in a locale that offers everything and nothing all at once.
America was built and saved by those dreaded hoards that stem fear.

Let them in- America needs saving once again.

Dear Sapling

Maybe one day,
you'll be taller than me.
I won't be here though,
so you'll have to compare
to somebody else.

How much time will life take in all?
Your insides will have to tell.
But only if they kill you first,
or run some sort of future
scanner across your back.

"Give me that ball!" The kids
will hoot and holler, prancing beneath you
and on your wet ground.
Generations of birds will
make suitable homes.

Maybe one day,
none of these things will happen.
Because someone will
question: "What kind of an idiot
planted a tree here?"

They'll cut you down, dig
you out, leaving the hole in
the ground that I put you in.

The Paratrooper

Time stops but the figures before the man keep moving.
On and on they perform with lone purpose in mind.
The man finds his body in ritual too,
copying their every move, singing.
This is all a movie, played back slow, primed for editing.

The grumbling beast turns on its side,
just when the birds thought that particular section of the sky was safe.
The movement for another pass captures the man's stomach.
His will to ever say no again is gone.
The men in front of the line all hook up and chant.

He turns to see that nobody is there to copy his movements.
Nobody is there to push him out if he doesn't seem to have the action required at the door.
He is the last in his line and the time is soon.
He knows as the other men near the door show an inch on their fingers.
All echoed by the lines of the willing.

The fear inside of him is so great that it reaches absurdity.
Boiling over, he can only smile and sheer himself out of his physical form.

He examines his body, his gear as he hovers above himself.
He watches the man turn soldier walk and hand his lifeline to another.
Time allows only a trusting, momentary stare.

Exiting the door into a sudden free-fall, intense wind steals the man's lungs.
Broccoli and toy trucks morph into a pause for judgment.
The soldier's mind can only whirl through the many decisions he has made.
Did he need to bomb that test? Did he need to take her out? Did he need to buy that car? Those and other certain events have driven him into this life, into this panic.

Will it end? Will he perish with the adrenaline soaking in his blood?
No. A snap of his torso gives the soldier hope.
His eyes look in wonder straight up at this moment's only love.
He can only guess this violence of body surely must mean survival.
A Canopy, a Savior, a Prince.

Work must be done now to ensure the rest goes well.
Proper descent is only up to him and the ritual he remembers, wait.
The soldier catches a peak of the horizon,
the beautiful reality meeting him at his same human level.
Eye to eye, mesmerized to be equal to the Earth and the Sun.

The spectacle has captured only him, is only for him.
His eyes follow the streaks of light to the ground,
past the tops of his trusty boots, an act the ritual warned against.
They said he must never ever look straight down as he has now.
He forces his head back to the horizon, his eyes must not betray the work.

The soldier pulls with all of his might this way and that.
Combating the wind with his silk savior.
He looks to the trees for permission,
the sign to release his only belongings to the feared below.
Down the ruck zings on a line, stopping far enough under his feet.

The time is coming soon, his eyes no longer an equal with the horizon.

"Be loose! Be loose!" the soldier cries only to himself, his feet and knees together.
Mantra, mantra, all the way down,
he can anticipate no more.

"Oomph!" The air leaves his body as he rolls to counteract the hit.
Tall blades, crisp and sweet, had no idea he was coming.
A reassuring fraction of a second without swelling pain is taken as litmus.
That is all the soldier needs to know he has survived.
He cackles, playful as a child, the spilling parachute covers him like a blanket.

The Mercenary

Cut our enemies down with that blade in your hand,
Screaming, "We don't think you live in this world."
You seem to have rascaled out despite the roof that you burned,
Holding on to your innocence, yet somehow still ready to go.

The visions you experienced previously were that of a paupers.
Inconsequential, you will not purchase your way out of luck.
The need to cut and grind, feeling the roots in the sands,
Remember, they will bleed you first and turn you to dust.

Reach toward the heavens, take the business at hand.
You do realize, the legs you post upon are caught in a rut?
Dig out underneath, travel out to those terrible lands,
Be the gavel, speak stern when the time comes to push.

All we need is some Chaos for you to feel free.

I am the Designer, the Ruler of Lands.
I choose you for this job, over me.

Advice #2246: Shaper, One of Them

Be careful Friend,
There is enough of that substance to melt your brain.
Smoke hovers all around, you Dragon.
Be choosy when you throw the spark.

Please, do not consume much too much.
Your mind will become flaccid, appear easy.
Try and not forget what you came for, you Lizard.
Staring at your shoes, neither happy nor sad.

Days may go by, dreams will fill your freedom, remember them.
Do not care, for habits are on a strict schedule though you are not.
Hours may dwindle and soon, time for rest, Princess.
Fight the urge to carry the routine, or drowning in dreams will be all that you know.

Find within your soul the loose grip,
Feel how your body stretches the wood and leather.
Release yours, into and through the eye, Archer.
How busy your day will be, throwing real arrows.

People older than you worked harder, yet had less time. How?
Do not ask how, they did not grow with you.
When thinking of them, you may find guilt, Rue.
Throw this to the kiln, use it all to your advantage.

Switch your input to purge, care to receive nothing.
Produce, think of using time to your advantage and rest with austerity.
Do not guess how long you were caught in the trance, Apprentice
Someday you will be a Shaper, One of Them.

THIS IS A DESTINATION WHERE TESTOSTERONE FLOWS

Where Testosterone Flows

It is and has been our own little world where the dust falls only for the purpose of being swept.

A quality wood and concrete palace, anchored in steam. We get away from it all for a while; see what activities lay in the sapped fields of mechanics and woodworking.

This is a destination where testosterone flows and the only talk is that of manly deeds: fish that grew in size since they had been caught last summer, tools bought at a bargain that seemed to have lost their way, and the miraculous repair of lost causes.

The smell of sawdust fills our noses, little gathering crumples creeping inch by inch away from the pile that sits near the table saw, their mother.

We know exactly where we are just by looking down at the identity-crisis floor that is covered with dirt, grease, dust, wet of melted snow, and the occasional oil spill here and there.

This grime may not be cleaned, no matter how many times the floor is swept, the friendly dirt and dust remains, residue of the past.

"Nothing needs to be perfect, this is just a garage," my father says as I try to remove a serrated edge with a belt sander off of the side of an old door-turned workbench.

There is a massive clutter of tools near the vice that were never quite put away during the long winter months. The idea of putting things away is not known to us here. After all, we may need them later.

What is known, however, are the tasks and projects that are to be held off for the spring season.

Airless bicycle tires, a broken bird feeder, wind chimes, fishing reels-all waiting to be fixed. They lay in a bundle near the old wood stove which breathes just enough heat to take the edge off the remains of winter.

But before all those virile tasks can be accomplished with, of course, the extra step of due process and priority, it is time to do some early spring cleaning.

"We'll start with the workbench," my dad says as we both gaze toward the pile of tools, formerly known as a workbench.

"Well, then again, we are due for a good break, how about a Coke son?"

It's almost sad to leave the great smell and sounds of the garage, but we definitely need a break.

As we head inside to the comforts of the sofa and a rerun, the sweet smell of sawdust and purpose leaves us. All that is left behind is the grime on our work boots, taken off gingerly in the mud room.

Yet, we always know that we must return. There is seldom a lack of chores and puttering to be done that require man power, rugged innovation, and the loyal shelter.

Best Intentions

We have not visited our dreams in quite some time
Together we had big plans, wanted to change our world and be different
Our children would eat real foods, have real names and grow to be real people
They wouldn't watch TV, play video games or grow to hate others
We wouldn't crush their hopes or make them addicted to possessions
Lofty goals for a young couple who were soon to be parents

On the L train, there were kids with mohawks who ate granola with their parents
We used to laugh at their moms in coveralls, wearing a nose ring, sometimes
But secretly, we were jealous, we have been controlled by our possessions
Those hipsters on the L may have been rich and fake, at least they were different
We don't know if they were genuine or how they acted toward others
Regardless, I admired them for their efforts, by not being like most people

We would name our son Blueberry, call him Blue, raising the brow of our people
We would be unique and not repeat the atrocities of our parents
We would give up certain luxuries, live simple, trade one for another
We would indulge in the status quo, never, well maybe sometimes
Build a creative harbor for our children, that would make all the difference
Loving each other and our offspring, no one treated as a possession

But a strong understanding of the task at hand, we did not possess
Diapers, baby food, appointments and medicine don't change for special people
Expectations of others, in the end, make yours different
Pressure from the outside world, especially from our parents
Forced us to focus on survival and forget about our dreams in time
It is all my fault I think, I made poor decisions with money, among others

We fell into the trap of the common American household, with so many others
Our daughters have been given a stream of gifts, have learned to expect possessions
My persistence for originality has subsided with a uniform worn over time
My mother would argue that we are more capable than most people
That we are much better off than most cookie cutter parents
But we are both stranded, fulfilling common expectations, there is little difference

I was surprised by your lack of stamina to hold the flag of stubborn difference
Who do I compare you to? The hippie heart of a pretty yet simple other?
What right do I have to question your ability to parent?
Don't we all desire? Don't we all need possessions?
I can't question you, I am not that great of a person
I teeter on the edge of self-destruct, I squander away the family time

Sometimes life is not real to me and the different dream leaves me possessed
We have done well though, thwarting the pressure of others, fostering future people
I wish you told me you still believed the dream, but sometimes I am too absent to be
A good Dad

Advice #2247: The Now

Leave us to soil about the whole day with our hands in our pockets
Eat steel, breathe with ambition

Find a new, modern way to spin the caper
Jab once, then release the fury

Us to move about with bits of sonnets, garbled in our brains
Leave now, take care

Eat your own words and tie in your oasis
Someone else to blame

Send a random attack from your high ceilings
Rain down, rush with the energy

Send us a sign, a big cool to cast across the water
Rake the forgotten moments

Not enough will come from those of the past
Gorge now, sleep well

Dance in the lunatic shadow of tomorrow and bleed the before
Don't control your anger

Coil and snare over and over, repetition eases the mind
Feed your notions of intent

The now is not a selfish feeling, it simply rapes the future
Seldom regret

Motor

Warm Rain
Easy Sweat
Go

Room for Few
Friends

Laces Up
Squeeze In
Tree Smell
Fuzzy Dice

Feel the Breeze
So Content
Low Hum
Take this Hill
Fast

Smiles Abound
Exhaust Drone
Look Outside
Directions

Common Guidance
Stop for Food
Cup Holders
Trash Goes
Here

Laughs with Radio
Crisp Angles
Mirror Paint
Top Down
Breeze Bankers

Common Ground
Here and Now
Freedom

To Meet this Day to End

The first rocket screams through the clouds down into the dead of night. Impact.
A hard knock thuds with echoes of shrapnel.
Fighter jets destroy the wrong building, their own men yell and sizzle.
Starched green national force uniforms hang their heads low and consider.
What to do now with the enemy who is fortifying the true target?

The foreign technocrats try at it again as the sun rises, success is met.
The attempt cracks the impenetrable structure as insurgents clench their teeth.
Along the outer wall, men lay in wait while the ghouls under the earth starve.
They suffocate and tend to their own wounds.

Brilliant, luxurious homing mechanism
Lay waste, spill a pool of familiar blood
Crushing the hope of a clean invasion

Raised on savagery and tutelage of a strict kind, the defenders swear to slay any
breathing who would risk advancement.
The aggressors themselves desire swift victory and want no loss of life from those
brave who dare enter the tunnels.
Yet not a man amongst them volunteers to be the first to go, face to face with the still
breathing yet dangerous enemy with nothing left to lose.
The crafty who wait devise a plan to break the cold pipes leading into the structure.
Saturating the dry earth, men drown and freeze.
Some scratch and claw underneath, never to give up.
Few escape wet with weapon and fight only for death's sake.
The last holdouts are butchered and hung on display.

Third-party civilizers watch
until they blush. To meet this day
to end, Liberators in a foreign land

The Invasion

When you're in the crush mode, you're deep in the dredge.
Look across these front lines,
You'll never see us break this march.

Past the point of no return,
Say we'll never meet again under the shield, look,
Here comes an arrow.

We must be getting closer, closer to the edge,
The toughest part lies just in this short distance.

Spread your wicked lies on the innocent,
Pool your filth and sewage straight down the river.

You don't even know what you've created in the bog,
Just try and destroy what you've made by your own hand.

All you know is extravagance, wine and decadence,
Comes through so ugly on the other side.
Look through the mirror, see us again, again, again.

You should have built some stronger walls,
This enemy has crushed them.

Your archers can't sling an arrow,
With their bodies twisted and their arms broken.

The Chaos, it takes over,
It spills through your people.
Where is your king?

Follow me, it seems the king's escaped to the crypt,
Weaseled down, left his men to die.

Don't cut his eyes out, don't cut his eyes out,
Need for him to see what he's done, what he's created.

Follow me, follow me
We're going down to a place not strange to us.

The Bachelor Party (Fred Wed Fast)

As stated Fred wed fast
Set caves as caves
We ratted Fred out
We broke open wet cases
We gassed tea
Bros set tramps as traps
Friends all fared fast
Fred eventually caved
and Revved sad
Dew was vast
we were Bare
and Tasted raw
but the Carts were saved
and Fred felt rested
Fred released
Fred was Freed
If only for the moment...

The week next
Altar time
We all were there
Recovered
Promises to keep
Promises to break
Plenty of time to
Pack and go home
Go Fred! Go!
We all secretly chanted
Just a tad
Marriage pillage
The "Proper" set up
Painstaking words
Proposal conclusion
Here we come
Fred panicked
Patience everyone gave
Purchase of thought
Steady, steady Fred
We all prayed
We all waited
Fred puckered
Kissed before the words!
Nervous laughs
All around
Fred was married Anyway

Lucky

The worst is to win early
Pores on the nose and forehead act like a sponge
Blankets of significance fall upon your invisible aura
All of this is controllable-the beast can be tamed only by special you

Before you ever began, rules were set-boundaries
Good parameters too-so solid
Brackets broken down by the wind of an early vic
You might call yourself a success and simply walk away now

Nobody can-all set in-a fortified castle of magnificence
Tonight is your night to place more wages-wildly based on previous profit
Time to realize the drinks are free
Chin goes here, on this pedestal-take one-no two on the mouth

Cannon fodder crumbles the outer walls of the crypt
Look how perfect the towers once were-could be again
Rush to rebuild, opportunity only takes a moment-a flash
Wouldn't want to miss out on any chance of success

Those around treat currency as a play toy
Money has all the meaning in the world, yet none at all in these halls
How wonderful to work in this way-using magic and chance
Forget the guilt of hungry mouths to feed back home

Victory could be made here and now-home could have it all
How easy it is now-in the future-to get more cash to spoil, try again
The establishment must keep the lights on somehow
The house always wins, so bet on black

They Hired Me to Sweep the Floors

They hired me to sweep the floors.
No responsibilities other than that, no chewing.
I swept those damned floors for I don't know how long.

Then 'ole Jeb taught me how to do my first weld,
somewhere in between the cracks of a long day.
Nothing official, just a "hey, lookie here kid." No change in title yet.

I was still sweeping the next morning-never knowing when my big chance would come.
I imagined the moment they would say go and I would snap right to.
I'd be the best damn welder they ever saw.

My big chance took a while to roll,
nothing as expected-just another check on learning really.
I was all nerves and real eager too, almost showed off my forever broom hands.

Instead, I ended up doing both jobs.
A Sweeper and a Welder-so proud.
I never whistled so much on my way to work-swinging my lunch pail.

One day, the boss called me into his office and confirmed-
'ole Jeb had taught me to weld and I didn't let 'ole Jeb down.
Boss man barely looked at me when he gave me a fifteen cent raise, heck I didn't care.

No more sweeping for me.
From then on, I learned all the welding types there was.
I watched sweepers come, sweepers go-no promise, no fire.

I did every job on that factory floor.
I learned for myself, I got to know me.
Nothing's more satisfying than the challenge of building.

I run that company now and I truly know the difficulty-
Searching for a Sweeper-a doer with fire instead of an overeducated malcontent.
This task is near impossible, the worst part of my job.

I find I have better luck when I post to the job boards "paid internship" instead.

Balance

For every burn there is indeed tasty output,
a feeling of desire left met. The ash is forgotten,
an embrace without reciprocation. A jaundiced
caterpillar gulps down what he can
and lifts up to the heavens, but only when
the time is acceptable for his taking.

How many sturgeons would rise out of the
water given wings? Their old bodies could easily
tell them otherwise. To the fragrant notes
all smiled at, above and spoken with or without
delight. Even they are smoother, slick in warning.

When the cardinal sees his star, so manic
and so forgiving. His lover washed away again,
no care, no promise to return.
How much will become of such items as they are categorized,
beyond the notions of intent.
Forever sucked into a feeling of being, a massacre on stage.

Bruised beyond sarcasm,
without so much as a whimper,
the changes and mocking of the expected
can only be derived,
from the negative.

Forget the principles of everyday life and standard
adaptation. With all the colors and sound about him,
the chipmunk can learn, overcome obstacles
and treachery. Nature will undoubtedly do
the deed for him, masking forgiveness with a letter.

Man has always turned a blind eye to the obvious.
He forgets nature and her overcoming achievements,
her balance and forethought. Patience and gratitude
have seldom been in a man's stomach, nor his heart.
How long has it been easily written, that in the haze of abandonment,
a child would overcome the need for a parent?

Too little time has passed for friends
to not be reunited. After all, a kite cannot forget
the string, nor the speaker the pedestal.
Too long forgotten are the prettiest that grow wild,
without seed or frustration or currency.

Too menacing are the eyes of destruction,
waiting for the line to be forever crossed in the sand.
Oh how the building blocks of time fold upon themselves.
A judgment is made with only one clear answer:
it does not allow for absolution of any kind.

Tear at the wolves as they would shred and gang,
cluster without the desire of harm to the paw. Rip open
the core of regret, give the correct answer with no second
chance, no alteration to be had but the ultimate choice.

The future is forever without metal wings, they
are not in this inventory and will fold
into the paper with ease, no sound.

Marc D. Crepeaux has worked as a burdock slayer, lawn mower, ice rink attendant, janitor, umpire, baker, sandwich maker, tree planter, pizza delivery boy, cashier, real estate flunky, warehouse goon, song writer, musician, personal assistant, bookseller, artist, bellman, doorman, concierge, construction stooge, paratrooper, night watchman, taxi driver, taxi company owner, worm farmer, vehicle prospector, linguist, substitute teacher, tutor, entrepreneur, private investigator and writer. He lives with the esteemed Mrs. Dawson and two daughters in Rome, Georgia.

Mads Bender has labored as a lawn mower, bus boy, cook, waiter, clerk, media specialist, smoothie maker, health food store supervisor, graphic designer, musician, barista, paratrooper, product designer, graphic artist, propaganda designer, UI/UX Developer, product manager, project manager, freelance developer, writer, editor, retail manager, taxi dispatcher, salesman, farm hand, roofer, painter, marketing professional, entrepreneur, and philanthropist. He and his wife are in the habit of collecting hobbies and window shopping for dogs in Athens, Georgia.